This book is dedicated to my Mum and Dad who were married for 71 years. They cared for me sacrificially during the first few years of my life and throughout my childhood, enduring years of worry and anxiety. I am eternally grateful. As I write this, my Dad is still alive, aged 93. To my 3 brothers, who never seemed to complain about me being the centre of attention due to my medical needs and have always believed in me, a big thank you. To my Godmother Sheila, who prayed for me incessantly and took her responsibility as Godparent seriously and finally, to all Mums and Dads bringing up small children with complex medical needs. May you know God's strength this day.

CONTENTS

REVIEW

It has been a privilege to read John's very real and insightful reflection on his unique journey of recovery through trauma and addiction. I was moved reading his story: he writes with honesty, vulnerability and compassion and peppers his writing with poetry that will touch and resonate with many hearts. His testimony holds much wisdom and will encourage and inspire those struggling to face their own addictive behaviours, helping them to begin their own journey of recovery.

Deborah Chua
Director Authentic Business Group

PROLOGUE

Everyone has a journey which is unique, with precious gems and gold appearing as a result of God's refining in our lives. My own journey is no different, a miracle; it testifies to God's protection and my family's love and care. This is a book I have been wanting to write for many years, a very personal story which I am glad to share with you, and it involves others in a very intimate way. I have no desire to be selfish and I want to be sensitive to the feelings of those around me, those closest to me, so I have taken my time, wanting to get it right. Even now, I check all my writing with family and friends, valuing their input, and my desire is that my words-bring healing, rather than pain.

I also am aware that in one sense recovery from life-controlling behaviours never finishes, so we are always on a journey. Can I guarantee I will never entertain old behaviours in the future? No I cannot, neither, I believe, can anyone else. It's not a promise anyone can make or be expected to make. This kind of careful reality check is helpful; in fact, it is when we forget about the journey we have been on that the dangers reappear in and around our lives. This said, I now feel I am at the point in my life where I am ready to share: my desire is to point others in the right direction and for them to be honest with themselves and with others and to embark on the recovery journey. There is a massive link between childhood trauma and addiction and I hope that as I share my own story, others may be able to make this same link for themselves or for loved ones.

I no longer seek to be put on a pedestal, whether of my own making or as a result of others adulation, in fact quite the opposite. For me personally I have experienced being put on a pedestal and have crashed down to earth with a bump. I approach publicity with caution, understanding my own weaknesses more than ever. I do not seek the emotional highs and lows that being in the limelight brings and I am content with a steadier ride.

In saying that, I have had a recent creative explosion; designing expressions and writing poetry have lit a fire within me to share my heart. Others have said how the expressions and poetry are benefitting them, so in this personal account I have attempted to integrate my poetry, some of which is of a very personal nature with my life story. I hope I have succeeded.

Please enjoy.

1. IT'S NOW OR NEVER

There was great excitement in my family at the birth of their 3rd son, born at our family home in Orpington, Kent, England. It was a Friday in December, the year 1960, 9 months exactly after Easter Sunday and my parents with much thought named me John, which means 'God's Chosen.' It's a name that is special to me, which I wear with absolute certainty and, knowing now what I know, it was fitting that Elvis Pressley's "It's Now or Never" was top of the UK charts. It must have felt like that as I was born, a massive step into the unknown; especially as a few days after birth I was diagnosed with a Congenital (1) Hiatus Hernia, a condition that was re-diagnosed later in my life as a Congenital Diaphragmatic Hernia (CDH) (2). It was this diagnosis that has shaped my whole life. Even now approximately 50% of children born with a CDH die in or around birth and it is the 2nd biggest killer of infants and children in the UK.

Way back 60 years ago they had little knowledge of the condition. The doctors said to my parents, "if he can survive until the age of 2, he can have an operation at Great Ormond Street Children's Hospital in London." After 2 years fighting to survive, with constant projectile vomiting, keeping down very little food and severe stress for my family, I was operated on to correct abnormalities of my stomach, oesophagus and diaphragm. My parents prayed for me and I am sure that the operation's success, which was at the cutting edge of medical knowledge at that time, was related to the prayerful petitions of family and friends. My Mum and Dad often recounted that there was another child in the hospital with me at the same time and the operation on him was not a success. My oldest brother remembers leaving me in the hospital and my screams could be heard along the corridor as they departed, whilst my mother also recounts that after the operation, due to the severe discomfort, I used to sit bolt upright in a chair crying. I had a thoracotomy (3) with a pencil thin scar halfway around my body. It was a fight for survival and I spent my growing years getting food stuck in my oesophagus due to the muscles there not working properly (4) and I had to chew everything thoroughly. On occasions, larger lumps of food became lodged in my oesophagus, resulting in my being tipped upside down or thumped on the back almost daily in order to dislodge them. On 2 occasions, I was unable to dislodge food stuck in my oesophagus and had to have tubes inserted into my throat to forcibly push down the offending items. I remember having no sedation and finding the whole episode very frightening as a child. The 23$^{rd of}$ November 1974, when I was 13, was one of those occasions: I was watching a football match at Elland Road. In much distress, I spat out my saliva onto the terraces for the whole match, trying to stop the build-up in my oesophagus, and I even remember the match; it was an obscure game between 2 neutral teams in the FA Cup 1st round, (Farsley Celtic vs Tranmere). The childhood trauma I suffered in those early years was immense. I was always last finishing at mealtimes and my brothers were long gone. Whilst my Mum and Dad cared for me so much, and my brothers put up with me being the centre of attention, those early days in my family were quite Victorian, with little touch, so my rough and tumble play fights with my brothers and friends, as well as the daily thumping on my back was the extent of the touch I received. Nonetheless I was a happy and very determined child and, remarkably, I excelled at cross country running, despite being behind physically. Every year I sat cross-legged on the front row of the school photo, with my white, blond hair and blue eyes, and I was the smallest in the class due to my difficult early years and late developing. I longed to be sat on the chairs or stood on the bench of equal stature to the other boys, but it was not to be.

"The automatic repression of painful emotion is a helpless child's prime defence mechanism and can enable the child to endure trauma that would otherwise be catastrophic. The unfortunate consequence is a wholesale dulling of emotional awareness." Dr Gabor Mate

Unlike my friends, who talk of a conversion experience for when they first found faith, I believe that I grew up from an early age with a personal knowledge of God and a deep childlike faith. My gratitude even as a small child was deep-rooted, and I felt special, believing that God had his hand upon my life. Every day of my life I have woken up with a choice to make: how am I going to approach the coming day? My wife will tell you I am most definitely a morning person and I try to listen to the song in my heart when I wake up, as it often speaks into the day ahead!

This first poem is about this daily choice.

CHOICES

In life there are choices
The first for me at birth
My bodily deformities,
Were they to give me worth?
They could have defined my lifestyle,
My attitude each day.
Maybe the world owed me,
Someone has to pay.
I had the choice of bitterness, anger with the world.
My tongue could be a poisoned arrow, full of curses hurled.
But my parents called me John,
A name they carefully found.
Chosen of God to hear a very different sound.
With gratitude I grew, despite the early strife.
Glad to live, a happy child, my thoughts were full of life.

To exist itself was precious,
Every day from God was new.
A lifestyle of gratitude, filled me through and through
But the choice still remains, at the start of every day.
Bitterness or gratitude
Which will be the way?
I've too much to be grateful for,
So many reasons to live.
Allot of life before me allot of love to give.

It's time to live again.

Trauma in childhood can create a fragmented foundation for an individual for the rest of his/her life. The way we are raised and the sense of security it creates impacts the emotional, and sometimes physical path, we as adults take.

Dr Gabor Mate: A hurt is at the centre of all addictive behaviours. It is present in the gambler, the Internet addict, the compulsive shopper, and the workaholic. The wound may not be as deep and the ache not as excruciating, and it may even be entirely hidden— but it's there.

(1) A disease or physical abnormality present from birth.

(2) A congenital diaphragmatic hernia (CDH) is due to the abnormal development of the diaphragm while the fetus is forming. A defect in the diaphragm of the fetus allows one or more of their abdominal organs to move into the chest and occupy the space where their lungs should be. As a result, the lungs can't develop properly.

(3) A thoracotomy is a surgical procedure in which a cut is made between the ribs to see and reach the lungs or other organs in the chest or thorax.

(4) When food is swallowed muscles in the oesophagus contract, contributing to the rhythmical peristaltic movement along

the digestive tract.

2. CAN YOU SEE ME?

I always questioned as a teenager how my congenital hiatus hernia would affect me as an adult and wondered if they had mis-diagnosed my condition. I remember emotionally asking my parents, "What if they missed something?" Although I was happy as I grew up, those teenage years were difficult. I was incredibly shy of girls and barely ever even spoke to them and was embarrassed by my lack of physical maturity. Except for during sports, touch was minimal and, despite being everyone's friend, I lacked intimacy. This is a poem I wrote which speaks into this time in my life.

Invisible

Shhh, can you see me hiding,
through the crowded room, I'm gliding.
Bothering no one, eyes not meeting
And when they do it's oh so fleeting
Please don't address me, don't engage.
A frightened rabbit in a cage
A little awkward, I don't exist.
Hidden in a shrouded mist.

I must survive, never offend.
A happy child an easy friend
Angelic eyes and white, blond hair
Always shy but ever aware
of my childish looks and bashful persona

Everyone's friend and yet a loner.

Pleasant to all but lacking touch.
To talk to girls was all too much.
My fear and panic, I ran away.
If only I had the courage to stay
The childhood trauma and lack of touch
The combination proved too much.
Seeking comfort to ease the pain.
Medicate to keep me sane.

The controlling behaviours, a sinister song
Deep inside a need to belong.
A call from the deep, a tender sound
Acceptance and love must be found.
A rhythm of hope for this broken soul
Pain and healing to make me whole.

It's time to live again.

My need for touch was very great during my teenage years and I found solace in my Friday evening Christian youth group called Crusaders, and by going to watch Leeds United 'home and away' twice a week. From the age of 10 onwards, I would travel across the City to Elland Road. Even now I can remember the bus journey on the number 1 or number 4 bus from Headingley to Beeston, overlooking the stadium. The buzz would start way before the game was underway and the adrenalin would build up even as I thought about the match in the morning. From the age of 13, I would travel to the away games, to grounds that are no more: Maine Road, Ayresome Park, Roker Park and Highbury, to name a few. It was in this context that I found the sense of belonging I longed for, and whilst I still had a very strong faith, I didn't feel comfortable in the religious church setting that we attended as a family. I remember communion being passed along the row, and being missed out because I was a child!! I was indignant with rage - "who are they to judge?" but wouldn't show it. I knew my faith was strong, how could it not be, as God had his hand on my life. I also went to a religious Church of England School and, as often happened, thought completely differently to everyone else. The whole school was encouraged to take communion, which flabbergasted me: I would wonder, "How can that be, when many of the children don't have faith?" When I watched the Religious Education teacher, who was also a Priest, swigging down the wine left over in the goblets, it just confirmed to me it was a nonsense. I presumed the wine was alcoholic and he was teaching children later that morning. So, I refused to take it. Around the same time on a Sunday in church, I would watch as downy feathers fluttered down from under the roof as we worshipped, and was awestruck that angels were in the building: could nobody else see them?

The physical changes into adulthood happened embarrassingly late, as a result, I personally believe, of the healing and restoration process going on in my body, and these changes were accompanied by much emotional pain. My parents loved me greatly but never talked about puberty and sex, probably because they were unable to due to their own upbringing, so I was left alone with my emotions and thoughts. I had feelings for girls but would never dare say because of my fears, and no-one would be interested!!! Despite getting a B grade in my GCE (General Certificate of Education) English, to everyone's surprise except me, my English teacher said my thinking was not mature enough to take it at 'A' (Advanced) Level, but the truth was, my view of life was alternative to others around me, and I didn't accept the normal analysis of the literature we read in class. My world was a parallel world and my train of thought went down different corridors and came up with alternative conclusions. Instead, I took Maths and even went for extra Maths lessons but failed miserably: I hated it and I was no good.

We had a great family life and I was a happy child. Mum and Dad always took us away twice or three times a year on fabulous holidays in Scotland, the Lake District and on summer camps. I regularly went fishing with my Dad, who was an expert fisherman but would never admit it and I loved spending time on the banks of lakes and rivers catching tench and trout. I played outside every night: football, cricket, messing around on bikes, garden-hopping (don't ask), and my 3 brothers, like me, loved sport. My Mum was a star: I remember one Christmas we were all given different items of football kit and we went out to play. We came back plastered in mud from head to toe, but nothing phased her, we all stripped off in the kitchen, the clothes went into the wash and life went on. For me though, looking back, maybe a sister would have helped me: had I had one, perhaps she would have encouraged me to overcome my shyness and subsequent feelings of isolation.

The patterns were there already in my life, the trauma and the isolation of my first few years, having to keep the barriers up, as my little body was operated on by well-meaning surgeons, and the subsequent lack of touch, and that same isolation was further reinforced as a teenager with my late physical development.

Dr Gabor Mate: *"What seems nonadaptive and self-harming in the present was, at some point in our lives, an adaptation to help us endure what we then had to go through. If people are addicted to self-soothing behaviours, it's only because in their formative years they did not receive the soothing they needed."*

As an adult I used to question where was the evidence of the life-controlling behaviours that I battled with, when I was younger as a child? Did they just appear in my late 20's?!! Now I understand if only in part, now I see.

Roller-Coaster

My behaviour started at the age of 10.
All week planning, culminating when
the turnstile clicked and I entered the ground.

Sweaty odours as I looked around.
Heartbeat racing: I took my place.
The chase, the buzz an emotional race
Extremes of tension, highs and lows
The final whistle exhaustion shows.
Drained of energy I went on my way.
To return again, another day

In my 20s I went to church
From meeting to meeting I did lurch
The emotional energy just as strong
The chase, the buzz, just as wrong
The addictive charisma, the joy and fun
I couldn't exist I had to run.
With childhood traumas I had no hope
The highs and lows I couldn't cope.
The dangers were there for this broken child.
For comfort and solace, I went wild.
Hidden behaviours my dark friend
The traumatic pain had no end.
At an early age I learned to block
Extremes of emotion ran a mock.

Now I prefer a steady ride.
From emotional extremes I tend to hide
Steady away I prefer to go.
I want to let the others know.
To cope with extremes is a lesson to learn.
The highs and lows I no longer yearn.
Over time a new path carved out
Steady away I'm reluctant to shout.
I don't seek attention; I don't seek fame.
You don't even have to know my name.
Gradually, slowly I will rise.
And when I do it will surprise
For I've been hidden for too long

I've begun to sing a different song.

It's time to live again.

3. UNIVERSITY

My 'A' level grades were low and I started the process of applying to universities. One of the applications was for a BSc Joint Honours degree in Environmental Plant Biology and Geography at Hull University. This was before green issues were sexy although the Ecology party was running in the local elections. I arrived at the interview looking like I had been swimming and was soaking wet because the weather was awful. I think those on the panel felt sorry for me, and it's funny what you remember but, rather embarrassingly, I had bought a new black chequered jacket and found myself wearing the very same design as one of the panel members. During the interview I asked, if they were to offer me a place, would they consider me taking a year out to do voluntary work for a charity based on an old Thames sailing barge on the Essex saltmarshes. Wow, what a response I received: "Saltmarshes, saltmarshes!" they exclaimed!! As it turned out, it was one of the panellist's specialist subjects!! I think that was the masterstroke that won me the place and in hindsight the very best outcome for me.

I wish I could share accurately with you the smells and sounds of living aboard an old Thames sailing barge on the Essex saltmarshes. The halyards clinking on the masts of moored sailing boats in adjacent berths, water lapping against the sides of the barge when the tide was in, the paraffin lamps hissing as they shed light into the master cabin and the creaking of the timbers, as if some mystery person was walking up and down the deck as the barge settled on the mud twice a day. It was a magical year for me living on board 24/7, hosting mainly teenage groups, some from difficult inner-City backgrounds. We also hosted environmental groups and church groups, many of whom were staying so that they could learn to sail in the Wayfarer dinghies the charity had attached to the pontoon at the stern of the barge. It was a Royal Yachting Association accredited centre and by the end of the year, I was instructing sailing, not bad for a city boy with no previous sailing experience. I used to hitchhike down from my home in Leeds back in the days when hitchhiking was safer. I have many stories to tell of the times I hitchhiked including sharing the back seat of one car with a very large St Bernard dog, slobbering all over me, whilst on another occasion, jumping in the back of a van and finding numerous festival goers on hallucinogens, I had a question nagging me: was the driver under the influence? I almost asked the driver to stop so I could get out. My year as bosun was voluntary except for pocket money and I was the only staff member living permanently onboard S B (Sailing Barge) Memory. When there were no groups staying, I was alone on the marshes: sometimes when the tides were high I rowed home at night, the phosphorescent glow shimmering in the tidal waters as I dipped the oars in and out of the water and I could tell you when the tide would be in by looking at the moon. I needed that year so much, and I don't think I would have coped with university without it - at least I could now hold a conversation with the opposite sex!! Looking back, girls tried to get close to me but I wasn't ready, I kept my distance, sometimes embarrassed by their physical maturity compared to me!!.

At the beginning of the new term, I travelled the short journey from Leeds to Hull and my parents dropped me off outside the door of my university accommodation: it was a terraced house - the university had purchased several streets of houses called 'The Avenues.' I knocked at the door and was greeted by a guy called Peter, a mountain of a man with a skinhead cut and earrings! I can remember recoiling back a step and trying not to feel intimidated: the University had put me in a house with mature students, most of whom were ex-union representatives, studying politics and with some very left-wing ideologies. I survived their sometimes-brutal attempts to tear up my faith and had some interesting discussions with them. I remember going out to the pub one evening with them and they lined up beers in a row for me to drink!! It was a test and they were looking for my reaction. I think I shocked them when I got up and left - I had no other way of coping with the pressure they were putting me under and leaving alcohol undrunk has never been an issue for me, I can take it or leave it! Later that term my roommate changed and the university sent another student to take his place!!! This new guy arrived and soon left: maybe the spirit in my room was a clash for him? For some time, posters promoting "Vote Satan and the SATANIST party" had been going up around the campus and in the students union for the forthcoming student elections. Well, what do you know, the guy that put up the posters was the guy that had moved in with me!!! Interesting!! To be fair he didn't have horns and he was very normal, just very confused. I realised maybe I could speak to him as I knew him a little and the posters, which were large and bold, were upsetting a lot of people. I bumped into him on a bus travelling along Cottingham Road outside the university and I warned him that he was dabbling on the edge of the dark arts and that he needed to stop because it wouldn't do him any good. I'm not sure what the outcome of my words was looking back, but I said what I felt I had to in the only way I knew how.

I also remember on my first day at university I went for a walk around the campus and there were some year 2 students messing about playing football. I approached them to join in and overheard one of them saying that they were meeting for a serious match at the sports hall the following day. I decided to turn up unannounced and gatecrash much to their surprise and they invited me to play. I felt so lucky, I somehow managed to join the team that subsequently won the inter-mural league and cup for 2 seasons. God was looking after me, or that's what it felt like. Rightly or wrongly, one of the reasons I chose the degree was that it got me out and about, going on numerous field trips. The most exotic was Tenerife, paid for by the university, whilst others included a trip to a tiny Island off the Scottish coast called Canna and to New Galloway, which is Robert the Bruce country in Southwest Scotland. Overall, I enjoyed my time in Hull, immersing myself in the Christian Union and playing football and table tennis. I never had a girlfriend throughout my time at university: not only was I still shy of touch but I had Victorian rules going on in my head. These rules included: "the first girl you go out with, you must marry," and rules about what was acceptable in terms of intimacy before marriage, and what wasn't!! It was weird: I was certainly no film star, in fact, the antithesis of that, but girls arrived at my door upset about this or that saying they couldn't return to their student accommodation, and wanting to stay. Perhaps they felt safe with me? Anyway, I had rules and I never allowed it. Did I miss something or did my rules keep me safe - at this stage in my life, I probably think the latter, as I was in no place to cope with a physical relationship.

4. WORKING IN ADDICTION

Even after 3 years at university I still felt very naïve and fresh faced, so I made a rather drastic decision not to pursue teaching even though I was offered a place at Bath University for teacher training, and to commence working at a 'Christian' rehabilitation centre instead. This was a deliberate attempt by me to get some life experience, for I felt I had been protected by my parents as I grew up and had lived in a fairly sheltered Christian home. Luckily, or maybe unluckily, my year on the saltmarshes and the references they gave were enough to convince the charity to take me on. Even though I was on the staff team, I lived at the centre, and when I retired to my room at night I used to cry. I felt very broken, as the words that the residents spoke as they tried to handle emotions hidden by alcohol and substance misuse for years were like hammer blows which I took personally. I was reading the Bible one evening on my own, when some words jumped out at me from Galatians 3:v13, "Jesus became a curse for me when he died on the cross." I understood in that instance that the words the men spoke were not aimed at me but aimed at Jesus and he was able to take them. From then on, every time hurtful words were spoken, I consciously thanked Jesus that he took those curses. It was an invaluable lesson to learn so early on in my time working in the recovery field. I was still fresh faced though and knew very little about drugs and rehabilitation. It was as if the residents at the centre who were very streetwise could jump 6ft and I could only jump 3ft 6 inches!! I felt I would never be able to hold my own and jump the same height as them, the gap was so great. Whilst pouring my heart out one day, I heard a voice in my head, and I believe God was speaking to me, saying "Tomorrow John, we will jump 3ft 7, you and me together, then 3ft 8 then 3ft 9, and one day you will be able to jump 6ft." Phew!! God was with me, I could relax, and take it one day at a time!!

I knew little about recovery from drugs and alcohol, and the programme the centre heralded was that they tried to encourage the men to drink under supervision in moderation!! Wow, this was disastrous: times have changed and enough is known now about addiction to realise that anyone addicted to anything finds it extremely difficult to control their usage once they have started. For the alcoholic, alcohol triggers the pain, and the craving for more increases. It was not a good start to my life working in the recovery field.

However, not all was bad - the centre was in the Lancashire countryside and I was ready to meet a girl romantically, and, one day, some friends invited me to the Lake District along with another of their friends. Whilst I now had other female friends, at the age of 24 I began dating for the first time.

After 2 years at the centre, I was invited by my old youth leader to be considered for a full-time post as youth worker at a large Baptist church back in Leeds. I had to attend a barn dance at the church and then, after giving a presentation, there was a vote by the church members, to decide whether they wanted to employ me or not. My tactic was to woo the older ladies by asking them to dance with me; not that I could dance, but it must have worked, and I was voted in. What an answer to my prayers, as I was desperate to leave the rehabilitation centre. I worked at the church for 3 years, my long distance relationship keeping me 'safe' from the advances of other ladies and girls in the youth group. As at university, girls arrived on my doorstep, but my strong Victorian values shielded me. I remember a specific occasion when a girl arrived at my door saying she was 16 yesterday!! I knew what that meant, my resolve and boundaries were tested, but thankfully I managed to stay strong (1). It was around this time I went on a sponsored walk, in aid of Cystic Fibrosis, if I remember correctly. I climbed the highest mountains in Wales, England and Scotland: Snowden, Scafell Pike and Ben Nevis, one after the other. Snowden was glorious sunshine, Scafell Pike, very wet and at night, and there was snow on top of Ben Nevis. It was a memorable achievement and, apart from missing the coach home to Leeds from Fort William and having to sneak a lift on the Bradford bus instead, a fantastic couple of days. Life was very active despite my difficult start to life physically and, towards the end of my time working for the church, my fiancée and I got married.

We both enrolled on a training course attached to another church in Leeds and in time I went into a leadership role heading up a new church. We lived on a council estate which seemed to be going through a very difficult time. Life on the estate had both extremes, extreme darkness including house fires, broken bones and suicides which affected the team, and remarkable healings. I had a compound fracture to my tibia and fibula bones in my leg playing against the police at 5-a-side, and was in plaster for nearly a year, and we lived in a maisonette block up 2 flights of stairs. One day we were trapped in our apartment by a fire in one of the maisonettes beneath us, and the prospect of being lifted down a ladder by firemen with a full cast on my leg was not appealing, however the fire was put out and this wasn't needed. We ascended blackened steps with the smell of smoke on the way to our front door for many months after the fire but this was typical of estate life, drama around every corner. We regularly as a church went out onto the streets worshipping in amongst the maisonettes and high-rise buildings, and there was a path that meandered its way through the estate in and out of the tower blocks, which locals called the spotty path due to its black circular paving stones. As as we worshipped, the music wafted into the residents' homes. Sound travels upwards and even at the top of the very highest buildings our singing could be heard. On one occasion, on a neighbouring estate, one elderly lady living in a very high tower block commented that it was like angelic music coming through her window. She responded, and started attending the church that met in the community centre regularly, becoming a motherly figure for some very broken souls.

There are so many more stories I could tell, however a few come to mind. We used dress down as a team and after praying would knock on specific doors. On one occasion, two of us knocked on a door and, after introducing ourselves, the lady became verbally very aggressive, full of expletives out on the landing, and all the neighbours could hear. After listening to her saying" God hasn't done this for me and hasn't done that," we departed, but, trying to leave on a positive note, I said, "You know the good thing is, you have a relationship with God, it's not a very good relationship, but at least you know he is there." Some weeks later, we decided to return and knocked on the same door: the lady answered, and to our surprise said, "Come in, come in." I asked her what had changed, and she replied, "Now I know you care." It was a massive lesson for me: things are not always as they seem, and she had given us a hard time because she was testing us out. When we returned, we passed her test. After that, we visited this lady and her neighbours many times. Around the same time, I remember praying for another lady on her front doorstep after she shared a dream with us that she had had the previous night: she testified that she was healed instantly of terminal cancer when we prayed. The dream seemed to prepare the way for our visit.

Around that time, I had a confrontation with 2 men in Leeds City Centre who picked me out in a crowd outside McDonald's and specifically came over to me to harass me. I proclaimed my faith as I was sure this encounter was spiritual and they immediately went on their way up the street bent over double and coughing. Before Briggate was pedestrianised, there was a bus queue of people very close by who looked at me as if to say, "what did you just do?" A good friend was with me and he stood back as the 2 guys approached me: he understood it was not a strong physical presence that was needed but that the encounter was spiritual. On another occasion we decided as a church community to clean up the local beck that ran through the estate. It was a disgusting job, full of everything imaginable, old electrical items, rubbish bags and more. As we were cleaning, a team from the local council paid a visit to the beck: they did not know we were there and the reason they were visiting was to discuss the poor condition of the stream. No one had paid any attention to the beck for years and they were so impressed with our efforts. Was this coincidence or did our cleaning pave a way spiritually for the tide of neglect to turn?

However, despite so much going on, my life was empty and it was difficult for anyone to get inside the protective walls I had put up since I was a small child. I found I couldn't cope with the emotional highs of leading a growing congregation on an all-action estate and there was only one way off the pedestal I was on and that was to fall off. My own church leaders found it hard to get close to me and as I now know the inability to make close friendships and the difficulty coping with highs and lows of emotion are both adult responses to childhood trauma.

FAME

The chemical rush the Adrenalin flow
The temptation of success of being on show
The pressing danger fame can bring.
The highs and lows can often fling.
You around, perpetual riding
Pedestal heights never hiding.
Then down you crash what a fall,
the pain so great for one and all.
Do not believe what people say,
to maintain the momentum every day.
A place of solitude you must find.
A place of quietness for the mind,

where chemical rushes cease to fire,
Different pathways need to wire.
Jesus found that solitary space,
a place alone out of the race.
With self so comfortable, at one, at ease...
no need to perform no need to please.

So, practise retreating away from the throng,
learn to know you've done no wrong.
When you escape from the rush and chemical high,
a place to laugh and talk and cry.
At home with self, a sign of healing...
a peace, a joy, a familiar feeling.
As you commune with your father, strength you take,
new hope ahead is what you make.
As you return to the crowd and take your place,
better equipped to run the race.

It's time to live again.

My time leading the church came to an end as I started to battle
with life controlling behaviours. It was all very subversive though,
and hidden from view, and no one talked about such things
without making judgements, which brought me more shame.
I spent a few years working as a postman which I loved but
continued to have the most outrageous, false comments made to
me by church people around me, and my world seemed to be
falling apart. As well as the hurtful words that were spoken, those
in leadership also said they found it difficult to get alongside
me, probably a fair comment and something said regularly
throughout my life. I now understand that along with child
trauma issues often comes a difficulty in forming attachments.
If only I had known that then, it would have made sense of a
lot of things. These comments acted as a catalyst and I prayed
as I had done before in my life, "God help me." The next day,
a letter dropped through my letterbox inviting me back to the
rehabilitation centre I had worked at before and I went back into

addiction work, living on site in a lovely house with my family. I was older now, better equipped and felt very at home working in the addiction field but I was in denial about my own life controlling behaviours, not accepting I was an addict and that even though my behaviours were non-chemical, I was just like the men I worked with.

"Addiction is the search for oblivion, for forgetting, for the contortions we go through to not be ourselves for a few hours." (Keith Richards).

"Our brains are wired for connection, but trauma rewires them for protection, that's why healthy relationships are difficult for wounded people!" (Ryan North).

It wasn't long before my own journey progressed and I was deputy manager of a supporting housing project in Preston; however, as well as my own personal battles, I had big questions. "Why do churches always send addicts away to a residential setting to get recovery, why don't they offer a solution in their own locality?" After all, when addicts have maintained their recovery, they have shown great honesty and have stories of recovery to share in the local setting, yet they often never came back, choosing to live near the centres where they started out on their recovery journey. The church was missing out, communities of recovery in the local setting were desperately needed, but I didn't see this happening.

It was then that I got the chance to apply for a job in Bradford, managing a structured day recovery programme attached via a charity to a large Anglican Church (2). At the interview, they gave me the opportunity to bring up any of my own personal battles around addiction but I didn't have the courage to be totally honest. The programme was a 12-step programme (3) and clients committed themselves to coming into the project 5 days a week. It ticked all the right boxes for me and I was accepted for the job and I loved working there. Structured Day Recovery as opposed to drop-in or residential rehabilitation was a new concept in the

UK at the time. Those in recovery could tackle issues as they came up each day when they arrived at the project and the centre had a good reputation. As it grew, we had about 25 clients in recovery at the same time, motivated to change and committed to attending the daily programme 5 days a week. The first session on a Monday after the weekend away from the programme we called "checking in." It was a chance for the clients to feed back how their weekend went. I remember one Monday a new client was on the programme and he shared about how the voices in his own head disturbed him. I responded to him by saying that the centre was a safe place for him to bring his voices, and as I said that, another client stood up and pointed directly at me. "My voices are scared of you!" Well, fortunately, such confrontations were not commonplace and I was able to defuse the situation and arranged to chat and pray with him after the meeting. There was a strong sense of belonging which recovering addicts need and I had a fabulous team around me and a community of recovery started to build up in the locality.

My family and I now lived in Bradford and life was seemingly good. I came into work early one day with a colleague and found a literal black shroud wrapped around the whole building. The centre had a reputation for changing lives and those dabbling in occultic forces didn't like it. We unwrapped the shroud and broke the power of the curses that were spoken: seeing lives changed is a spiritual battle. I loved my work and had some memorable days out with the clients. On one occasion I organised a sponsored event with experienced qualified mountain instructors accompanying us and we climbed 4 of the highest mountains in the Lake District, one after the other, Scafell Pike, Scafell, Skiddaw and Helvelyn, a memorable achievement for everyone who took part.

I have learnt over the years that many of those with addictions, life controlling behaviours and non-chemical addictions tend to live compartmentalised lives, trying to keep their addictions under control and out of the public eye by attempting to restrict the behaviour within a certain quadrant of their life. In fact, appearances could suggest the very opposite of the damage the behaviour is causing, with public areas looking polished and manicured. An example of this is the way a resident in a rehabilitation centre might have a perfect bedroom, training shoes lined up neatly and shirts immaculately ironed and hung. Whilst learning self-respect and cleanliness is a good thing, the perfection in one room can give a false sense of everything being OK, both to the individual and to others in their immediate network of friends. In reality, our lives are holistic, with an ebb and flow between the rooms of our existence. Personal and work behaviours cannot be separated and habits and church life overlap. Sooner or later the addictive behaviour will spill out causing damage and chaos elsewhere.

BOXES

Those suffering addictions compartmentalise their lives.
Trying to build boxes to help them to survive.
Life controlling behaviours closeted away,
the pain kept in a corner to come out another day.
The other rooms look perfect, portraying peace and hope,
the shoes are lined up clean and spaced, "look how well I cope".
It's all a show for self and friends, as if they cannot see,
the childhood pain stuck in the corner, the property of me.

Life cannot be boxed there's an ebb and flow…
between the rooms in your house joy and sadness go.
When you lock your pain away, it breaks out in other spaces,
The careful hiding doesn't work, to appear in public places.
The embarrassment and shame rears its ugly head…
from within its box the pain breaks out,
be careful where you tread.
I cannot judge or pick out, the addict, you or me,
We all have pain locked away to this or that degree.

A single canvas can be painted as you try to live as one.
A tapestry with no walls has only just begun.
Openness, honesty and sharing,
not the time for comparing.
The journey ahead no one else can measure,
to embrace the pain and find the treasure.
Unique to you but travel with friends,
who you travel with just depends.
On open hearts and an honest soul
across the river and your goal.

It's time to live again.

After 2/3 years working for the charity, my own issues came to the forefront again: non-chemical addictions are powerful and not spoken about in many churches with openness and honesty. After chatting things through with the trustees, I chose to step down from my position managing the project. My behaviour was not acceptable, so with great sadness I resigned and handed on the reins to someone else.

This next poem speaks into this subject.

SELF-DESTRUCTION

In life there are patterns for everyone to see
The ebbs and flows, highs and lows, the things that make up me.
I didn't plan to self-destruct it just kept on occurring,
I could feel it coming from afar, my mind just kept on whirring.
The 'success' and 'fame' life was flying,
I expected the fall there is no denying.
Success and me didn't marry,
the emotional high I couldn't carry.
I couldn't cope with being paraded,
with recurring behaviours, I then traded.
I self-destructed with my dark friend,
the familiar pattern had no end.

My friends were left with confusion,
he did it again it's no illusion.
The hurt and pain were there to see,
the destructive cycle surrounding me.
I needed to find a different way…
a steadier path, a brighter day.
I no longer want to be parading,
'Success' and 'Fame' masquerading.
Highs and lows come as they will,
the occasional trough and even a thrill.
I'm now more prepared for the ride,
I meet my friends and then confide.
a solitary place to retreat…
with my maker I do meet.

So, can I ask don't parade your friend?
Those in recovery often tend.
To be showed off before the world,
their new 'success' like a flag unfurled.
But the very act can cause a high,
they look so great but hide a lie.
The fame itself causes pain,
to be paraded has no gain.
Except to promote false success
Leaving the friend to pick up the mess.
Parading addicts point to score,
They self-destruct as before.
I've worked in recovery for so long,
now I sing an honest song.

It's time to live again.

(1) I still took medicine each day to line my oesophagus: some
of the muscles that contract in a wave, called the peristaltic
wave, pushing food down, hadn't functioned since birth,
hence food got stuck when I was a child. When it happened,

it caused abrasions and swelling, making the oesophagus narrower and causing more food to get stuck. As an adult this rarely happened, due to the oesophagus being fully grown and wider.

(2) At that time someone with a prophetic ministry came to Bradford and spoke on the 2 famines in Genesis. In the first famine, in Genesis 12, Abraham took his family to a distant land to be fed. In the second famine, in the time of Isaac, recorded in Genesis 26, the first thing God said to Isaac was "don't do as your Father did." So, Isaac sowed seed into the parched land and it produced 100 fold. I applied this to the state of recovery in the church in the UK at the time: the church was always sending those wanting recovery away to a distant rehabilitation centre to find recovery, but God, I believe was saying to the local church, "you might feel parched and inadequate, but you do it."

(3) 12 Steps of Alcoholics Anonymous

1. We admitted we were powerless over alcohol — that our lives had become unmanageable.
2. Came to believe that a Power greater than ourselves could restore us to sanity.
3. Made a decision to turn our will and our lives over to the care of God as we understood Him.
4. Made a searching and fearless moral inventory of ourselves.
5. Admitted to God, to ourselves, and to another human being the exact nature of our wrongs.
6. Were entirely ready to have God remove all these defects of character.
7. Humbly asked Him to remove our shortcomings.
8. Made a list of all persons we had harmed and became willing to make amends to them all.
9. Made direct amends to such people wherever possible, except when to do so would injure them or others.
10. Continued to take personal inventory and when we were wrong promptly admitted it.
11. Sought through prayer and meditation to improve our conscious contact with God as we understood Him, praying

only for knowledge of His will for us and the power to carry that out.

12. Having had a spiritual awakening as the result of these Steps, we tried to carry this message to alcoholics, and to practice these principles in all our affairs.

5. RECURRING BEHAVIOURS, SAME RESULTS

I took a couple of jobs in the addiction field whilst searching for the way forward. One was disastrous, going for an interview to manage a therapeutic community but was offered the same level of position managing a rehabilitation centre in another city far away from home. I was tempted and accepted and, after going through the usual checks for managing a registered care home, I travelled down Monday to Friday to the Midlands, but it put extra pressure on my already strained family life. It didn't last long, in fact until I had the courage to step down.

Many who live in Bradford or Leeds identify strongly with one city or the other, however, for me, I easily move between them both. I had seen structured day recovery working well in Bradford, - a grass roots city, and I longed to see it in Leeds. I walked with 3 friends the 12 miles from Bradford city centre to Leeds city centre, praying as we walked, asking God to bring abstinence-based day recovery into the city. Then I wrote to the director of St George's Crypt working with the homeless in Leeds. At the time, they had around 150 people accessing their services every day, but, besides signposting, what were they doing for those wanting recovery from addictions? According to government statistics, 70% of homeless people have issues relating to drug and alcohol addiction and the director asked to see me, and as a result, I was paid for 6 months to set up an abstinence-based recovery project. When he spoke to me at the 'interview' he asked me, "how much do you want to be paid to set a project up!!?" I'd never been asked that before, like me, he was desperate to see it happen!

At that time, there was a big emphasis on numbers in treatment, keeping users off the streets and not committing crime, so many addicts were prescribed methadone. Methadone and harm reduction was the talk of the town around most of the drug and alcohol services, so setting up an abstinence-based recovery project was against the flow in the city. I went round these other services advertising our plans: I wasn't asking their permission but rather stating my intent, and I was fearless. I remember one lady working at another project asking me, "so you have actually seen people 'recover' and stay abstinent?" My heart went out to her, a lady with a big heart working in the addiction field, but who had never seen anyone maintain recovery because the emphasis was on crime reduction not on maintaining a lifestyle of abstinence. Visiting churches in the city, I promoted our plans: our heart was very much on being there to serve the city. The finance flowed in a remarkable way, both large and small gifts cascading down: it was the right timing and touched a chord within the city - they wanted this. I set up the project and later with the encouragement of the crypt, we obtained our own charitable status. This particularly helped with funding applications as we could then apply to the same trusts and foundations as the crypt without doubling up, and it also gave us independence whilst partnering closely. Whereas the crypt's mandate was homelessness, our mandate was recovery, and partnering together kept both of our visions focussed and clearer.

I have so many stories I could tell, however, one comes to mind. We had an older gentleman on the project and he came to me one day and said, "I manage to stay alcohol free all week but every Sunday evening I struggle and end up binge drinking." I asked him to recount his Sunday routine. He told me he got picked up for church in the morning, attending a lively meeting and going for a meal afterwards; he felt loved, and was loved. However, I knew from my own personal experience that those in recovery have difficulty coping with the highs and lows of emotions. The daytime emotional high and subsequent evening low was too much for him to negotiate on his own. I phoned up the church leader to discuss what could be put in place but my words were like a foreign language to him. This episode left me with questions: do we really help those in recovery by encouraging them to attend emotionally charged meetings and events and then leaving them alone to cope with the trough afterwards? It takes months if not years for a recovering addict to learn to cope with emotional extremes, developing new brain pathways. The rush of the charismatic meeting and the subsequent low afterwards was a difficult time for me personally in my own recovery journey; even now I no longer seek the emotional high but prefer a steadier ride.

I enjoyed working for the project I pioneered and established and there were many highlights. Having fun together and creating a sense of family and belonging is vital in recovery. As with the project in Bradford, we went on amazing days out and, on one occasion, we completed the canal walk along the tow path of the Leeds-Liverpool canal from Skipton to Leeds, 27 miles, a sponsored event in aid of charity. It was a challenging day and even harder than the Lake District walk, as the flat walking used the same muscles for the whole route, and the last mile into Leeds was tortuous. I learnt many lessons from the clients. I remember one time a client said to me he had a spare set of new training shoes. He told me he was going to take them to church on the Sunday evening and was sure someone would need them. On the Monday back at the project I asked him, "what happened?" He said, when he arrived, a man was sat on the church steps with bare feet, and the shoes fitted him perfectly. Wow, a lesson in faith for me and also a question. Would the man have been sat there if he had not exhibited faith? I headed up the project for a further 2 years before the trustees who I had appointed took me to one side, wanting to change my role. In truth, they were concerned about my inability to change my own addictive behaviours and wanted to give me space to come away from a frontline role. I couldn't imagine myself in a behind the scenes desk job in a project I had pioneered, so once again I chose to step down, leaving the charity to grow and thrive under another's leadership. Isn't that the way of the addict, the insanity of addiction, to keep acting out on the same behaviour, expecting a different outcome, but always getting the same result.

The pain in my life was immense and the sense of isolation tangible. I had caused a lot of hurt and my marriage was over: I went to live in Leeds whilst my family were in Bradford. I was unable to face the issues raised in me by my own behaviour. In addiction terminology, they call this, 'doing a geographical,' moving to another area to avoid facing your own issues. I became a private hire driver in Leeds for a year, between jobs and did my best to continue to be a good father to my kids. It was not an easy time for any of us. Below are 2 poems I wrote expressing the pain of the battle that many addicts face.

MY FOE

My foe, the very essence of who I fight against is who I long to embrace,
like a poltergeist following me from house to house,
the algorithm of my own familiar pain always disturbs me.
Targeted, focussed,
my own damaged self, causing destruction,
I yearn to stop running, to embrace my companion
at home together co-existing.
No longer unwelcome, a part of me,
the gold that it forms for all to see.

It's time to live again.

SELF

Every bone and sinew, my body screams to escape,
tormented by memories, the existence of which strive to shape,
the very essence of who I am, distressed and ill at ease,
how can I find rest my heart to please?
Bring comfort and companionship to my soul,
some fragrance of life to be make me whole.
The anguish of spending time in a crowd
of being alone or speaking out loud.
In case they find out the real me,
timidity and fear for all to see.
Communing with demons, seeking comfort from self,
The hatred and loathing is on the shelf,
for all to see, I'm going insane.
The instant remedy, to medicate pain,
engaging in behaviour, escaping me,
alone with self I have to flee.

The magic I seek at ease, at one,
the living of life has just begun.
To commune with self, no strife, content,
this is how life was meant.
Experiencing life at ease at peace,
the forgiveness of self brings release.
It takes time to live new fresh ways,
to find a way through life's maze.
To my soul, be gentle and kind,
sound and safe, of right mind.
The end is in site, able to live with me,
me and God, I'm feeling free.

There's no other treasure which I wish to own,
rewarding, inspiring I'm becoming known.
At home with self, igniting, firing,
the horizon nears, a complete rewiring.

It's time to live again.

I've heard people question many times how does the withdrawal from chemical addictions like drugs and alcohol compare with that of non-chemical or behavioural addictions like sex, love addiction (co-dependency), work, eating disorders etc? For me that is a very interesting question and I have personal observations. Withdrawal from a non-chemical addiction is powerful and the emotional pain can be immense; it must not be minimalized. Tremors and the shakes are quite normal when undergoing withdrawal from non-chemical addictions. Whereas the substances related to chemical addictions like street drugs and alcohol can be stopped, many of the things we are addicted to in a non-chemical sense are necessary to live a normal life; so, someone suffering from an eating disorder cannot stop eating food, sex is wholesome when in an appropriate relationship, we all need to work. etc. If touch, even loving touch triggers emotional pain, is it realistic to expect the person in recovery to stop all touch? The person working through eating disorders may experience emotional pain as they sit down and eat, for some it is the eating experience in itself that is a trigger - can they stop eating? No!! So, withdrawal from behavioural addictions can be complex and support must be offered and provided for the individual. The withdrawals can be severe: I would describe it like you are withdrawing from an emotional pain that comes from within.

Non-chemical addictions cause a lot of pain and suffering, particularly to the family and friends of the person caught in the web of addictive behaviour. I recognise in my own life that my sense of remorse didn't match the severity of the pain I had caused others. On occasions, people said to me "You don't seem to be showing much remorse?!" In my mind, I knew that this is how it must appear to others, but emotionally I felt switched off and distant to how my life was panning out and the consequences that it caused for those around me that I loved the most. I now understand that another symptom of childhood trauma is to switch off emotionally from the events going on around: this is a survival mechanism that is taken into adulthood. This detachment or distance is projected on to others around and can come across like the person doesn't care. The person suffering from the trauma does not have the capability or capacity to lower that emotional guard and it would mean addressing the childhood pain that would flood to the surface. I would argue that this engagement with remorse takes time and is part of the recovery journey. To expect someone in recovery who is also suffering from childhood traumas to suddenly show appropriate remorse is not realistic. The lack of emotional attachment is also a contributory factor towards an individual's constant lapsing or relapsing back to old behaviours and a detachment from life can seemingly lessen the emotional consequences of returning to a previous or new addictive (cross addicting) (1) lifestyle.

POOL OF DRY TEARS

A pool of dry tears numbingly enveloped me,
an aridness of soul screamed from within.
Dry and chaffed by the prolonged drought,
childhood trauma had frozen my heart,
my own protective armour surrounding me.
If you look you can see, the first healing teardrops rolling down.
There was a time when one drop would have drowned me,
now, I find rest in the pool of tears forming on the floor.
Joy and heartache, delight and sadness,
each drop has a name which together bring healing.
Embracing the emotion which forms a backdrop,
every shade of life alive in me

It's time to live again.

1. Cross-addicting is when an individual in recovery stops medicating their pain on their primary addiction but takes up another behaviour or uses another substance addictively.

6. THE SECRET IS OUT

Around this time, I met a lady on a Christian dating site and we started seeing each other. We travelled between Leeds and Keighley 3 or 4 times a week and we couldn't wait to meet up. She insisted we were just friends for about 6 months and we took things very slowly. She was good for me, accepting me for who I am and never forcing me to share more than I was able. We had an embarrassing yet amusing coincidence on only our second date when we decided to go to a Chinese buffet restaurant in Leeds. As we arrived, all the men in the church I attended turned up: it was a men's night out and unbeknown to me they chose to eat at the same restaurant as us and at the same time, for some reason I had not read or had been missed out on the mailing! They had no idea I was going to eat there and thought I had gone to the restaurant to eat with them, and then met the lady I was with (who is now my wife) that evening!! I'm not that much of a smooth operator. We all laughed and if I intended to keep my relationship a secret for a while that was no longer possible.

Despite my brokenness, I was head hunted once again and invited to head up a national charity training and equipping charities and churches who work in the field of addiction. Their training material gained University accreditation and I enjoyed my role delivering training and tutoring to diploma level. I loved traveling around the UK but I didn't find delivering training easy. It was great when speaking from the heart with enthusiasm but I found subjects I was not passionate about difficult to deliver. The trustees encouraged me to give my time to a charity called ISAAC

(International Substance Misuse and Addictions Coalition) on a voluntary basis alongside delivering the training and equipping. I loved building ISAAC networks across the UK where Christians working in the addiction field could serve, encourage and equip one another and I was integral to hosting exciting conferences up and down the length of the country. It was a symbiotic relationship between the 2 charities: on the one hand I gave my time to ISAAC and in return I was able to promote our training throughout the UK. ISAAC is unique in that it does not have its own therapeutic programme so can work across the different recovery brands and projects without being considered a threat. I helped several churches and charities establish day recovery projects and amazingly found myself equipping others and delivering training internationally. In Myanmar I led a workshop at the ISAAC Asia conference on day recovery, reaching Christians working in the addiction field in countries like Bangladesh, Myanmar itself and Pakistan and whilst in the Philippines I delivered training to an exciting project in Cebu City.

Around this time, I also established a franchise to equip and enable churches and charities to set up a day recovery programme which I still have the permission and authority to roll out.

My partner is Filipino and was in the process of gaining British citizenship. After 3 years of dating, we got married: we had a fabulous marriage blessings ceremony organised by my wife's sisters and brother on a beach in the Philippines, and basically all we had to do was turn up. My only regret was it was my first time in that country and even on my wedding day some of the cultural differences took me by surprise. I think a visit prior to getting married would have helped prepare me more. Quite soon after we had 2 children, and I was an older Dad bringing up kids for a second time.

My own mum made me aware of a saying in her family that the men die at the age of 53. In my 52nd year I started getting chest pains which seemed to abate with stretching, and I was getting tired walking short distances. One of my brothers commented when we had to stop walking so I could catch my breath on the way from the car park to Elland Road, and at the same match I was trying to stop myself from getting excited because when the adrenalin flowed I was getting chest pains. This spurred me into action and I went to see my GP; I did not return home as she called an ambulance immediately. On my 53rd birthday to the day at Leeds General Infirmary I had 4 stents inserted into the arteries in my heart. The cardiologist called my chest pains heart attacks; however, I was grateful that the radiographer afterwards could detect no damage to my heart. After looking at my notes and the screen, he even questioned what procedure I had had done, as he could see no evidence. Once again I was sure God was looking after me, at the beginning of my 53rd year I was not going to come under the family curse.

It was at this time that my life took an amazing turn. I went to see my local GP and she was listening to my chest and decided to send me for a MRI scan at the hospital: she did not say why. During the scan, I could see the hospital staff pointing at the images with exaggerated movements and when they assisted me off the bed at the end, with great concern, I knew something was wrong. I went back to my local GP and she said, "It's good news and bad news." The good news was it was not cancer, the bad news was that I had a hernia in my diaphragm. An appointment was made with the Thoracic department at St James Hospital in Leeds. After attending a couple of times, I became aware that the senior consultant was not passing me on to his team, I thought it strange as others who I knew who had had a diaphragm hernia said they had endured a relatively small procedure to fix it. The consultant suspected more was going on than showed on the scan. My medical records from the initial operation at Great Ormond Street Children's Hospital 52 years previously could not be traced, so I will never know what more the surgeon knew about my body when I was a toddler. I noticed the word congenital appearing on my notes and he told me that he suspected the hernia had been there from birth. The hernia is a Morgagni hernia, and the reason I mention this is because this rare anterior defect of the diaphragm only accounts for approximately 2% of all CDH cases and is more difficult to detect.

When I went into the operating theatre, he found I had been living my whole life with a full loop of my colon in my left lung space, pressing onto my heart, and over time it had become fused to my diaphragm and to my lung wall. He was a very experienced surgeon and he was astounded. When he came on his rounds after the operation he was shaking his head as he spoke to me, saying, "it's amazing John". How had my body adapted to living like this and how had it stayed hidden all these years? That one day put my whole life into perspective and so much fell into place. I always wondered what an epiphany (1) was like; now I knew. My whole view of my life's journey changed in that moment, what a relief, it was as if a weight had been lifted off me!! My questioning as a child was right, they had missed something. Dr Papagiannopoulos or Dr Papa as people affectionately call him had a great interest in my case and told me he thought he had just added an additional 10 years to my life and said I was to ring him directly anytime if I ever have any issues; thus far, all good. He also said that in his opinion my colon pressing against my heart had contributed towards my previous heart problems. My gratitude to God is immense, a common theme throughout my life. How I managed to excel at long distance running as a child with reduced lung capacity I have no idea and, in addition, the huge walks I went on throughout my adult life? I couldn't help noticing the parallel between the secret hidden inside my body and the hidden behaviours I had battled with all my life, however, now the secret was out.

Despite the surgeon saying before the operation that he expected to do a small 2-inch incision, I once again I had a huge scar halfway round my body on top of the previous scar. It was enlightening to experience the same incision as I experienced aged 2: without wanting to be gory, the surgeons cut through nerves and ribs to give sufficient space to work within the thoracic cavity. With my ribs moving around I felt a great discomfort and pain during my recovery, reminding me of how I must have felt as a small child. I sought to find others with similar stories. It was then that by chance online I discovered the CDH UK charity (The Congenital Diaphragmatic Hernia Charity) and I was amazed to find so many children born with the same condition. I subsequently learnt that each child's condition varies, but the common thread was that there were concerned parents and families doing their best under extreme circumstances to bring up the child to the best of their ability. I was directed to chat forums and soon realised that at times the parents were desperate with worry, like my own parents had been, and that each child, like me, was a survivor. Whilst there are those who are older with the condition, I have yet to hear of anyone my age, and, rightly or wrongly, I felt I carried a message of hope for some of those struggling families. Each year on my birthday I try and write words from my own experience to encourage others. One year about 40 families messaged me and one in particular said they read my words over their child as she was sleeping. Wow, very moving.

I consider my scars to be beautiful because they remind me of my journey and what I overcame and I do not regret being born with the condition, for out of suffering come pearls of great value. I am grateful it took so long for it to be fully diagnosed; would my parents have let me have such an active childhood if they had realised the true extent of my condition? They were so right to call me John, for indeed I am chosen.

THE SECRET

My body held a secret, hidden locked away,
refusing to come out into the light of day.
It shocked me when it surfaced and shocked the surgeon too,
the most eminent physician amazed through and through,

I've heard the word epiphany and wondered what it meant?
A moment of revelation, something heaven sent.
In that instant I viewed my life in a completely different way,
3 was 4 and 5 was 6 there's nothing else to say.
It all made sense; a light switched on,
the truth was out, the mystery gone.
The hidden struggles, I understand,
dangers traversed God's guiding hand.
The relief was massive, colour exploded,
the whole of me fully downloaded.

I knew for sure it's time to leave,
the old behind but give space to grieve.
I'd lived with the secret for so long,
needed time to sing a different song.
Years progressed I embraced the new,
the change in me was right on cue.
I don't understand the process, why I felt so free,
the missing piece, how it had burdened me.
I only know that the secret is out,
I'm free to run and jump and shout.

It's time to live again.

I came away from this period in my life with a growing sense of gratitude. To my local GP, who was the first Doctor in over 50 years to suspect something was amiss in my lungs and sent me for a scan. For the fantastic care I received from the thoracic team at St James Hospital, and to God my Father in heaven. Somehow, there was a divine timing to all these events: the stents put in on my 53rd birthday and even the fact that my CDH had been undetected up until this juncture in my life. It felt 'right' that I had lived a fully active life up to that point in time without knowing the truth of my condition but, also, now was the chosen time to get it fixed, for the pressure on my heart, lungs and diaphragm was increasing to calamitous proportions.

(1) Epiphany: A moment of sudden or great realisation or revelation.

7. RIDING THE WAVE

Running alongside my time working for the training charity, my wife and I, from the beginning of our marriage, started to host international students in Leeds on short term language courses. We rented a large 6 bedroomed house and with the permission and encouragement of the owner and his wife we took in students. It was an exciting time and we loved opening our home: during the next 10 years we had over 185 students to stay with us from over 35 countries. We have lots of precious stories to tell and friends we have made. There were the 3 girls from Hong Kong who were so excited when they arrived because they had seen a horse from the coach window being fed in a field, and later, instead of the usual 10-pin bowling outing with their hosts (us), we were able to go to the local fields and let them feed a horse. The same girls wanted to lie in the garden late at night to watch the stars as light pollution in Hong Kong prevents this. There was my friend from Turkey who, although a Muslim, when he left, said to me, "you are my spiritual Father" - what a privilege. And the lady from an Arabic country who at great risk came to stay with us because she wanted to experience family life. We spoke at length in the evenings about all sorts of issues which she did not have the freedom to talk about in her own country. So many special friendships were made with guests from all over the world: Japan, the Oman and Spain come to mind, but so many more as well. Our home was always a hive of activity. On a few occasions, we had Indians staying and I loved the breakfast curry smells wafting through the house as they made their own homemade rotis and curries; sometimes they invited me to eat with them, always a treat. Often our friends and family looked on incredulously at our lifestyle: for us, rather than being a threat, the cultural variety added to home life and to the education and life experience of our children.

Around this time, I started to develop a limp and began to use a walking stick. I had a hip replacement operation at Chapel Allerton Hospital in Leeds: the reason I mention this is the orthopaedic surgeon was surprised that my left hip was in need of repair, yet my right hip showed little sign of wear and tear. It was one of my sons who is a physiotherapist with a very holistic mindset who suggested that the congenital defects on the left side of my body might have caused all sorts of hidden stresses and strains, possibly leading to uneven loads and pressures, and I find it interesting that my CDH had an influence far beyond my own understanding, both emotionally and physically. My recovery was very rapid, this was aided when I learnt that my new hip from day 1 was fully load bearing, and this made a massive difference to my attitude towards the pain experienced as I learnt to walk on my new hip. As with my understanding of how childhood trauma has consequences later in life, a little knowledge can be really helpful in being a foundation block for both physical and emotional healing to occur.

During this time, I started to apply the lessons of recovery I taught others to my own journey. Firstly, I believe the most important lesson is that there is no recovery without emotional pain, although many will try to find a way including circumventing the usual therapeutic approaches. If you want a recovery free from emotional pain, don't set out on the journey, for there are no short cuts. Pain is necessary and something I have begun to welcome in my life and the journey is the teacher. I am learning to ride the wave as the pain comes, for I now know each wave will pass and leave behind gold and treasure, building resolve.

THE PAIN

I ride the wave, reaching a crescendo before breaking.
Every wave is consistent yet different, always making me feel like
I want to run away; but stay I must.
For the pain is a friend to embrace and trust.
Learn to ride and go with the flow,
enjoy the pain and take the tow.
I have learnt to ride because the wave will fold,
and the pain will leave and deposit some gold.
When the next wave crashes by,
I have gained some strength with which to try,
to ride again another day.
For each wave that's ridden makes a way,
leaves treasure and resolve within my heart,
pains healing touch helps me to start.

To live life again.

Dr, Gabor Mate *"The attempt to escape from pain is what creates more pain."*

Those that try to find recovery without pain actually invite more pain because the issues that need to be confronted in their lives are hidden away, festering underneath the surface, waiting to break out. I've heard many who work in the addiction field say that those who leave recovery early and go back to using their drug of choice have at least tasted what recovery is like. As is often the case I come from a different angle, in that every failed rehabilitation attempt can build disappointment and lethargy. In psychology, learned helplessness is a state that occurs after a person has experienced a stressful situation repeatedly. They come to believe that they are unable to control or change the situation, so they do not try, even when opportunities for change become available. Entering a rehabilitation programme is stressful and I believe with repeated 'failed' attempts at pursuing recovery, learned helplessness can happen within this setting. I think it is important not to encourage others to enter a programme of recovery until they are ready. Many times, people came for an interview to join a recovery programme I managed and were not accepted for this very reason, very often because a friend or family member brought them along before they themselves had the motivation.

I have friends who miraculously met God whilst in the depths of despair and, like the apostle Paul in the Bible, had a Damascus Road experience, yet even for them, the emotional pain of the journey of recovery cannot be avoided, for the pain itself is the vessel that brings healing.

I keep on learning that each battle is won with my very first thought and action. If you are a gambling addict the battle is won when deciding to not pick up the form guide, computer or newspaper at the very start of the process. Picking up the newspaper will trigger the pain and the need to act out on your addiction will multiply. For the sex addict the battle is won with those first thoughts, a glance at a magazine or the internet: don't start to go through the planning in your mind because this will trigger the pain and increase the craving, a vicious circle which gets harder and harder to retreat away from. I don't like the term 'love addict' because it's not love, but for those in a spiral of addictive relationships, including internet relationships, in a cesspit of co-dependency, don't be tempted to start the chase (1): take control and ride out the pain at the very first thought.

NON-CHEMICAL ADDICTIONS.

I talked to a girl on the internet, then I talked to three,
multiple conversations deliciously driving me.

It didn't matter if I met them, the chase is all I need,
hooking them, controlling them, the routine on which I feed.
My behaviour took me over, consumed my every thought,
a co-dependant cesspit, one I wasn't taught.
I fed them and they fed me, toxic through and through,
no tear shed as I let them down, moving on to someone new.
Nonchemical addictions so painful to withdraw,
a subject rarely talked about, a fast-revolving door.
I skipped my meals, I lost sleep, I was even late for work,
Life controlling behaviours round every corner lurk.
I see it all around, in friendship groups and churches,
hidden behind smiles, the pain and heartache lurches.
It's a sin, you must stop I hear the preacher say,
the judging words of others not offering a way,
to stop the behaviour, address the pain, honesty a must,
not just from me, from all, a way of building trust

I also see it paraded, accepted, even boasted,
co-dependant lifestyles honoured even toasted,
on the telly, in the press lifestyles feeding pain,
every colour of the rainbow driving me insane.
A new honesty is needed to address this lifestyle curse,
nonchemical addictions only getting worse.
Honesty from all, it's not about them and us,
passengers together, riding the same bus.
Life controlling behaviours affect us all, to this or that extent,
it's time for us to change, something Heaven sent.

It's time to live again.

At this juncture, I am impressed to mention the whole area of co-dependency which is a behavioural addiction and is rife in society and in the church. Co-dependency is when each person in a relationship is mentally, physically, emotionally and spiritually reliant on the other. This relationship can exist between partners, friends, family, within business or within a church and those relating are doing so in a harmful, dysfunctional way. The relationship is unhealthy and is a way of avoiding facing up to emotional pain. So, for example a pastor is meeting his/her own need to be in control of either an individual or a group and the individual/group are seemingly 'happy' to be the victim under the control of the leader. Both parties take up their role as an attempt to avoid underlying issues and associated emotional pain. Another example of co-dependency is in a marriage when one of the couple is an alcoholic and stashes drink away in hidden places and the partner, although knowing this, refuses to challenge in order to keep the peace. They are relating in a dependant dysfunctional way, keeping the status quo to avoid 'rocking the boat.'

In recovery, relapses will happen. I have learnt that whilst the relapse causes hurt and pain it is the response to the lapse or relapse that is the most important issue. Hopefully, the person in recovery and the family and friends around can see the lapse or a longer relapse as a stepping-stone to growth, not a final 'nail in the coffin' with no return.

Whilst some justify their behaviour because they are an addict, for me that is not an excuse for causing harm and pain to another person. For sure it gets harder and harder to retreat from acting out in a compulsive way as the cravings increase but for me the individual needs to develop the ability to take those very first thoughts captive before descending into a vicious downward spiral. 2 Corinthians 10: v5 We demolish arguments and every pretension that sets itself up against the knowledge of God and we take captive every thought to make it obedient to Christ.

THE DANCE

The prospect of the dance is so appealing,
the lifts and throws will leave you reeling,
the dance begins, I've not reached the floor,
the chase is on as I exit the door,
of my house, I'm on my way.

A choice I make every day.
Do I go or do I stand still,
good or bad my head to fill.
As soon as I leave, I feel the pain,
to dance with the devil has no gain.
The more I dance the pain increases,
My heart and mind the pain then teases.
Learning new moves, I get drawn in,
it triggers the pain; I just can't win.
Quick feet and partners to the fore,
a vicious circle to the core,
Make the choice, don't set out,
the only way, I'm in with a shout.
Grab that thought when I want to go,
Talk with friends let someone know.
For the dance is a monster, dark and deadly,
it's time to play a different medley.

It's time to live again.

Other questions I have had to ponder many times are the statements like "Once an addict always an addict" and even the dislike by some people of the term 'addict'. I find particularly in Christian circles many put up passionate arguments about these statements and terminologies. I could argue my point of view here but this is not the time or place, rather in my own journey I have reached the point where I am aware daily of a certain level of pain which in itself is an important admission. When I ignore the pain the danger of relapse is greater; I prefer to say that I am an addict in recovery. Whilst identifying myself as an addict in recovery, I believe everyone is an addict to one degree or another, for all keep on 'sinning' often in the same way to avoid emotional pain. So I cannot separate myself out from those with behaviours that are more socially unacceptable; we are all in the same boat in life. Is there hope for the addict? Yes I believe there is: through honesty with self and with others, there is a way through.

Dr Gabor Mate "What happens in the first four years of life has a profound effect on how we're going to be for the rest of our lives. Adverse Childhood Experiences (ACE) and unmet emotional needs are highly correlated with addiction and dysfunction. But he also points out that while those early experiences are highly influential, "They're not written in stone—they can be reversed."

(1) The Chase The rush of excitement and infatuation that certain relationships can spark may, for some people, kindle the desire to chase after that experience again and again. This may be reciprocated by the other person/s feeding a negative destructive co-dependency.

8. FINDING ACCEPTANCE

Understandably when patterns of behaviour run deep, and you have hurt a lot of people, it's difficult to accept yourself and find acceptance from others; there is great mistrust. For me, I have been grateful to be part of a church in Leeds that allowed me to heal at my own pace and had no expectations of me. The last thing I needed was to be put on a pedestal because that is the very last place I want to be; for me, there is only one way off a pedestal, and that is to fall off. I have a particular heart for those who have very public addictions and are also extremely gifted. We can all think of sportsmen or women and famous musicians who battled with chemical and non-chemical addictions. How difficult is the emotional ride of being idolised and dramatized and coping with the emotional fallout! The high of the concert or big game and being hero worshipped followed by the come down afterwards. Many times, I see the rich and famous being interviewed on TV about their personal battles with gambling, sex, drugs and drink and I question the wisdom of the interview. Fame and profile and the emotional high will be followed by a massive low, and an addict in public recovery must have enormous support in place to work through this without relapsing.

I have had many hurtful words spoken to me during my recovery journey, words of judgement with no mercy, words spoken from hearsay not from facts. I have even been told I was not welcome at a church, but I have realised over the years that those who judge others often have their own massive issues that they are hiding, whether knowingly or unknowingly. Now when I attend churches, I can see non-chemical addictions shouting out at me from the faces of some of those attending; who I am to judge?

I had the first line of this next poem pop into my head when driving; it was a personal cry that I desperately wanted to change. I wanted so much to write the poem as if it related to someone else not me, however I could not escape.

BELIEF

How long does it take to start again?
How long does it take to be believed?
Change can be a lonely place,
Mistrust the shackle in the race.

How long does it take to start again?
Familiar lies have been my friend.
To set my face truth to choose,
the deceitful friend I now must lose.

How long does it take to start again?
I look the same to my friend.
Days or years how long to face?
For truth to find a resting place.

How long does it take to start again?
Willing to change and make new friends.
For few of the old will believe what's new,
truth is living right in view.

So how long do you need for your friend to change?
To believe the truth of a life transformed.
One week, one year or maybe never,
it takes belief to travel together.

It's time to live again.

It was very recently that God met me in a dream and spoke healing words into my life concerning past hurts from words spoken by others. I realise now that the shame these words brought cast a shadow over me and only now do I understand that I was seeing life through cloudy glasses, that I only saw in part.

1 Corinthians 13: v Now we see in a mirror dimly, then we will see face to face. Now I know in part; then I shall know fully, even as I am fully known.

I love this next quote and it got me thinking to write a poem. Does the poem leave questions? Maybe so, but I hope it makes you think.

Dr Gabor Mate "The difference between passion and addiction is that of a divine spark and a flame that incinerates.

THE FLAME WITHIN

I could not help but notice the flame burning within him,
ferocious and destructive, uncontrollable in the way it scorched
and burnt the very fabric of the man he was meant to be.
I looked long and hard but I never once saw it extinguished,
always burning with the potential to be fanned into a roaring
cauldron at any moment.

I see there is a flame burning in you,
the passion within that drives and motivates to accomplish great
achievements,
the flame that others admire, flickering and making beautiful
impressions on the landscape around, touching the lives of those
that are lucky enough to feel it's warmth.

I changed my focus looking back at the man, tears formed in my
eyes and fell to the ground as I watched,

the dignity in the way he accepted the flame was enchanting.
For it is part of him, the very essence of his existence.
When for a moment he denies the flame's reality it roars into life,
with a wildness that flaunts its destructiveness.

I have finally accepted the flame in me.
That although the same burns differently to the flame in you.
I've accepted the flame won't stop burning.
It's futile for me to keep on yearning for it to be extinguished,
for the flame is the very essence of who I am, forever a refining
fire.

It's time to live again.

Finding an element of self-acceptance is essential; the poem
hints at this. I no longer fight the pain in me - the potential
destructiveness that burns - but I have accepted who I am. The
pain belongs to me; it might ebb and flow but I need to welcome
it and embrace it like a friend. For the flame in me is a refining
flame that makes me who I am. To fight the pain or to always wish
it would disappear is futile, in fact in wishing it would go away,
the tendency is to seek medication to hide it away. Medicating the
pain is different for everyone who is addicted, for some involving
chemical addictions like drugs and alcohol whilst for others non-
chemical behavioural addictions.

Even the apostle Paul was very real when talking about the inner
battle. It says this in Romans 7: 19 For I do not do the good I want
to do. Instead, I keep on doing the evil I do not want to do. There
was an acceptance of his inner state and the battle within, and I
believe this acceptance is essential as an individual moves ahead
in their recovery journey. To live in unreality is dangerous as our
defences will drop and we will fail to put in place the necessary
checks in our life to help us to remain free of our 'drug' of choice.
Yes, we can overcome, however overcoming must be rooted in the
reality of the potential for destruction within us. It is by God's
grace we can overcome, not through any power of our own, lest

any man should boast.

I am grateful that throughout my life I have had a strong sense of being chosen, that God has a special purpose for my life. In saying I am chosen I believe everyone is chosen; you are chosen by God because he loves you and because he loves who you are. He has a special purpose for your life. If you are unsure about this and are lacking that sense of being special ask God to reveal this to you, how he feels about you and the unique purpose he has for you in this life.

In some ways this next poem has a childish edge, but some of the most profound concepts can be found in children's writings and books. For me if I am to continue to walk the recovery road then that can only come out of an integrity and honesty of lifestyle, from a place of totally accepting who I am, including my strengths and weaknesses. The alternative is to white knuckle (1) my recovery by building boundaries and walls at every turn to keep me 'safe'. The idea for the poem came from a late evening walk in the local park, the sun was behind me and my shadow stretched out long and thin before me down the path. The image stuck with me.

WALKING WITH GIANTS

Today I walked with a giant.
His shadow stretched out ahead like an arrow pointing the way.
He had such presence when he walked, an aura that made those he passed stop and stare.
They loved touching his shadow hoping to catch something as he journeyed.
Everyone knew sometimes he was a grumpy giant and he didn't always get things right,
and everyone knew he had struggles inside, despite his happy smile.
But that's why they loved him.
because the giant was fully known.

They knew there was nothing hidden, which gave them confidence as he passed.
In fact, that is the very thing that made him a giant.
No physical thing that made him attractive,
no perfection that others need to attain,
Just honesty with self and those around.
I long to walk with that giant every day.

It's time to live again

I read this poem to a friend who I bumped into at Brimham Rocks in North Yorkshire as we had a family day out on Good Friday, and he reminded me about what the prophet Isaiah said about Jesus approximately 2000 years before his birth. Isaiah 53: v's 2-3 There was nothing beautiful or majestic about his appearance, nothing to attract us to him. He was despised and rejected- a man of sorrows, acquainted with deepest grief. For sure, a timely reminder of what a true giant is like.

(1) White knuckling Recovery

An example of white knuckling would be when riding a scary rollercoaster; just grabbing onto the handrails as tight as possible in a state of nervous anxiety, whilst waiting for it all to be over. White knuckle sobriety is in some ways similar to this. The individual is just using pure willpower and a set of rules to stay sober. It is like they are just hanging on, waiting for the ride to end. When first in recovery these rules and boundaries are necessary to bring a degree of protection and stability, however this is not a satisfactory way to live in recovery long term, and it can almost always be avoided.

9. MORE THAN A SURVIVOR

Over the last 5 years, my wife and I have run our own small business. This overlapped with our time hosting in our home in Leeds before moving over to Bradford during the height of the COVID epidemic. Every large city has a short stay community so we took out a 5-year lease renting up to 7 apartments in Bradford city centre and, with the landlord's permission and appropriate contracts, sublet through well-known booking channels. I wanted to challenge myself to use the skills gained establishing and heading up charitable projects to try and run my own business. We enjoyed hosting, attracting some fascinating guests, including those connected to all the big shows at Bradford Alhambra Theatre. The dancers from Miss Saigon and Lion King, lead actors in Hairspray and the Christmas pantomimes, to name just a few that come to mind. A number of times we got complimentary or reduced-price tickets, and on one occasion my daughter and I were sneaked in round the back of the stage by the lighting crew (who were staying in one of our apartments), to watch Matilda from the sound desk, a great view. It wasn't always straightforward managing apartments, as the 'twilight' community were always trying to book for activities relating to drugs, sex or partying, so we had to be one step ahead, keeping our booking procedures and protocols tight. We had families staying from all over the world, often visiting their adult children studying in Bradford and we aimed our marketing to attract families and international guests.

We were humbled that after 5 years of hosting, our rating on one well known booking channel was 9.1 out of 10; it wasn't because they were the most luxurious of apartments but because we always tried to go the extra mile. It is easy on social media sites and when writing an account of your life to present a perfect picture, however, in all honesty, hosting in our apartments had its difficult moments. During the height of lockdown, some guests slipped through our protocols and hosted a massive party and the invitation went out on the internet. Fortunately, we contracted in security to watch our apartments every night; the security lived in the same building, and through cooperation with the police and great bravery they sorted it out. On another occasion we had a masked gang turn up at one of our apartments threatening the occupants who ended up jumping out a second floor window to escape, badly injuring themselves. I understand now that it was drug related; however, over 5 years, incidents were few and far between. It has been a rollercoaster of a ride hosting thousands of guests, being gate keepers to our city and we are happy to have seen our contract through to completion.

We live in a society and culture where a great emphasis is placed on ownership; owning your own home and car amongst other things. Our testimony from the last 12 years hosting international students and from managing our own serviced apartment business is that a sense of purpose and fulfilment in life can come without ownership, the gifting God gives each one of us is not limited to earthly boundaries. God is not confined by our earthly status, I am indeed rich, rich in friendships, rich through embracing the different cultures and all that they bring, rich with colour and variety. I say to myself, "don't say you are poor because you are rich."

There are many of us here in the UK that have identified with the label of being a survivor for most of our life, it is rooted deep in our history. My parents talked about their own Fathers who fought in the First World War. My Dad's Father, George, was a machine gunner and survived the awful battles at the Somme, Passchendaele and Ypres but spent the rest of his life suffering the effects of mustard gas. My Mum's mother, Lillian, received a letter saying her husband had died on the battlefield and then, to her astonishment, Albert turned up unexpectedly on the doorstep at home. He was one of only six in his regiment to return from the war. Alongside this, my own fight to live resulting from the birth defects I was born with reinforced my own survivor identity. Whilst I don't deny that I am a survivor, if you remain in survival mode all the time it can limit your aspirations to staying within that framework. It is easy to adopt the attitude almost unknowingly that survival in life is enough. During the last year I have become acutely aware that I need to move on from this label, that there is more to life than survival; maybe even I can be a winner, whatever that means!!

SURVIVOR

Apparently I am a survivor, this is what they say,
bouncing back from life's extremes to live another day.
I see it in my family, the survival trait is strong,
World War I and World War II, a very familiar song.
I've heard it said a thousand times by well-intentioned friends,
the survivor word deep entrenched and the message that it sends.
I could be content with survival, at the age of 61,
but the reality of life is it's only just begun.
I'm not content with survival, there is more to life than that.
To dress in clothes extravagantly and wear a different hat.
My horizon is expanding, colours new in view...
now is the time for living, now I must be true.
To give and create expressions full of morning hope,
the message in my heart I no longer must elope.
When I limit myself away behind the survivor tag,
It's time to rise and run, under another flag.

It's time to live life again.

10. FURTHER UP AND FURTHER IN

To quote C S Lewis in his book, The Last Battle, "further up and further in." Isn't that what living life is all about? More adventures ahead, more mysteries to explore before us. As we feel we get closer to God in our journey, we experience more of heaven and in doing so, we realise how little of God we actually know and how much more of heaven here on earth we have yet to experience.

A year ago, at the age of 61, I enrolled on a course called Authentic Lives; their strap line is "igniting dreams, transforming lives." Through the Authentic Lives workshop, the aim is to awaken people to their full potential so that through living a more fulfilled life they can bring lasting changes to their own communities, workplaces, society around and circles of influence for good. I loved the course, relishing the chance to be more authentic to myself in a safe environment and I took up art for the first time since I was at school, creating my own expressions. Being brought up in a sport filled family with little room for creative expression it was a massive step for me. I remember clearly my CSE (Certificate of Secondary Education) art classes between the ages of 14-16 when most of the lessons were spent messing around. Everything depended on presenting a portfolio with at least 8 pieces of work, and with 2 months to go, I realised I had very little to show, so I spent the next few weeks cramming, including colourful ink drawings and ended up getting the top grade. Most of my work revolved around the presentation of colours. This is still true; I believe we all have a rainbow of colours within us to be expressed throughout life in a variety of ways. I have found expressing myself through my designs very inspiring and therapeutic. I have many artistic friends who throughout my life I have tried to support and promote and also, I ensured art therapy was part of the recovery programmes I established and managed. I thought this was my role, to be a catalyst to others. I understood the power of the arts as a communication tool, but I had not appreciated the powerful therapeutic and healing balm of artistic expression in all its many forms, some of which I am currently experiencing. As it says in John 12: 24 "Unless a grain of wheat falls into the ground and dies, it remains alone, but if it dies it bears much fruit."

This next poem explores the real me!! Maybe as you read you can identify with this, either fully or in part.

REALITY OF ME

When will I find the real me?
Was I lost as I journeyed alone?
Forced and shaped where I didn't belong,
worked and moulded into a vacant lot.
A lot that happened my way in life,
or perhaps I never even set out.

For the person journeying was an imposter
A dark actor brilliantly masquerading, using my gifts and entrenched in the drama.
I fully believed that he was me, as he wrote the script for all to see.

But my life took a turn, a twist, unforeseen in the stalls.
I entered the show with life and colour,
the final act, who would imagine?
Creative, flamboyant, dramatically different,
Proofread from Heaven to fit the occasion.
No part in the play for the intruder,
Banished and outcast, unmasked, forlorn,
I really have been reborn.

It's time to live again.

I feel fortunate to be exploring new parts of me hidden away for years; may I end my days continuing to explore new rooms in my mind and heart, not confining myself within familiar living spaces. This next poem is about this new landscape which is before me.

WILD HORSES

Can you hear me coming closer?
The sound of hooves, thundering and wild,
windswept and unbridled, galloping unchecked, mane cascading and flowing behind.
Is it right to try and change how I was created?
Born, never to be captured, never to be trapped and boxed into some religious conformity,
to serve tradition, laced up in a tight restraining girdle, hiding the risk of being different.
To end my days having only explored a small, confined space in my mind.

But I was born to worship in a huge creative landscape, born to explore the outer edges of who I am,
Born to journey and not stand still, born to experience danger, holding on only by my fingertips.
Born to display colour, black, dappled and chestnut,
every colour of the rainbow following the seasons of my life.
Born to be passionate, born to live life, bands of humanity travelling together.

It's time to live again.

Later in August 2022, one year ago, with the invaluable encouragement of others who had also been through the Authentic Lives course, I started to write poetry. I guess I knew that the ability was lying dormant within me but never gave myself time or space to develop the gift. If I am honest, I used my gift with words writing hundreds of funding letters for this or that charity, trying to present projects in a way that won over the hearts of those reading. I have so many stories I could tell of amazing provision. My desire in my poetry is to be honest, approaching issues including non-chemical addictions from a very personal angle. As with the artwork, I find the writing of poetry an amazingly therapeutic experience and am finding as I read it out loud that others feel free to share very personal stories from their own journeys, that for some have remained hidden for years. There are those that find my honesty disturbing, especially in religious settings, as I am touching on subjects that for many remain hidden and off limits. For me at this stage in my life I am happy if my poetry causes a reaction: subjects like sex addiction, love addiction, gaming, social media and gambling addictions amongst others cannot remain hidden and must be brought out into the light without condemnation and judgement.

I am a dreamer and have tried to listen to my dreams for the last 35 years. On many occasions I believe my night-time dreams have spoken truth into the situations in my life that I am facing. This next poem I based on a dream I had after I took up my artwork. I believe this will speak to many other people who are journeying as I am.

HOW LONG?

How long have I been silent, watching, listening, observing the signs around me, holding my thoughts like treasure of great value?
I've been patient for so long, a weary traveller waiting to cross.
Our separate journeys have merged together, a point in time, a holy place, a place of expectation and reverence.
Silent pilgrims, broken and honed by the distance covered.
Across the river the snow is melting on the towering mountain peaks,
fuelling the river into a frenzy, ever flowing wider and deeper.
Oh, to reach that place, to feel the fresh murmurings of spring, the Spirit of God blowing over the land.
Yet, separating us from the distant promise, the river flows, deeper and wider still.
To reach the other side involves faith and courage,
for none have ever reached the far bank when the river was shallow, in low flow.
The only way is by faith, jumping in, boldly letting go.
Now is the time, the moment to cross, to be out of your depth.
The melt water itself flowing due to the Spirit warming the land.
For there is no crossing without faith,
they run together hand in hand.

It's time to live again.

Hosting has been the recurring theme throughout my life; even as a youth worker, I was trying to provide an environment where kids could feel safe and have fun, whilst at rehabilitation centres the environment needed was to be a place where those in recovery could find acceptance and belonging. Both in Leeds and in Bradford we wanted to create an environment where guests in our home and in the apartments felt welcome, home from home.

What of the future, who knows? My aim is to become more authentically me, learning to live from what my heart is saying. I hope my art and poetry will move forward in tandem with others, not in an unattached, isolated way and I would love to see a recovery programme centred around the arts, but it is early days. I am becoming more confident of my own journey but as they say, "one day at a time." I look forward to my own designs speaking healing into individuals' lives as they have already started to do and also look forward to my poetry being published. I have begun to write 10 minute poems for people, sometimes strangers, asking God to give me words, and so far, these have been well received.

FAITH

Faith is setting out on a journey, not knowing my next step,
seeing my destination but not understanding how I will reach it
With each step I find space within my heart to move forward, not relying on past conquests.
The battle is with myself as I respond to the quiet whisper within, all around there are noises and voices jostling and pressing.
Faith leads me on a journey exciting yet terrifying to embrace, each courageous step putting down a marker for others to follow
It silences the murmurs of my own discontentment, leading me onward, the very act propelling me forward.
With faith my heart is a staging post, opening up a way for me to go and others to follow, a supernatural gateway of revelation and flow.

It's time to live again

I am beginning to understand that many of the things that were previously "no" in my limited world view, are in fact "yes," and my eyes are being opened to a stage that is more colourful and much bigger than my zealous, evangelical roots allowed.

WHEN I GROW UP TO BE A CHILD

I've never felt more like a child than I do right now,
It's true, the older I get the less I realise I know and what I do know
no longer weighs me down.
What's gone on before has lost its pain as if a line has been drawn,
the only thought in me is what lies ahead to press on towards the
goal.
My excitement for the journey is tangible,
my expectation is out of reach, way beyond the confines of
normality.
Faith explodes from within, wild pathways to tread,
colour, life and exuberance,
My provision for the journey ahead.

It's time to live again.

To be able to move on from the life of escape that childhood
trauma brings is a massive step. I have that desire to move on from
being frozen in time to embrace the future.

*"Trauma may lead you to build a life of 'escape'. But underneath is
the desire to unfreeze that part of you stuck in time and release it to
live all in." (J. Mike Fields).*

For me this has been a journey but to understand the process that
came with childhood trauma has really been helpful. Alongside
this knowledge revelation I have found the healing balm of artistic
expression and belonging to a group of like-minded people very
therapeutic. I am at that point in life of wanting to live all in, with
new adventures and pathways.

I also look forward to greater links with a global organisation
called Golden Doors, for whom currently I am an ambassador. For
sure, the area of my tent is being expanded and my knowledge and
understanding being challenged.

This last poem I dedicate to all the families and friends who have had their hearts broken by loving those afflicted by the curse of addiction and also specifically for those who kept on loving me through my darkest times. Thank you.

It is tough to love and to keep on loving.

GREATER LOVE

Love is to allow someone the choice to walk towards the precipice, knowing they might never return.
Love is to deny the urge to be the rescuer and to embrace the pain of a broken heart.
Love is to see a part of you suffering time after time and not to intervene.
Love is not knowing and still hoping whilst getting darkened whispers from afar.
Love is hearing lie after lie and still believing.
Love is to realise you are not the answer and point the way to the giver of life.
Love is choosing to live alone rather than being someone else's fix.
Love is not being the provider for another's compulsions.
Love is allowing pain to be the healer.
Love is never to stop praying and always watching.
Greater love has no one, than he lay down his life for a friend.

It's time to live again.

AMEN

Many of my designs and poetry can be viewed on www.GlobalHeartbeats.org

If you have been affected by the subjects covered in this story and need someone to share with, I can be contacted by e-mail on mybodyhidasecret@yahoo.com I do not claim to have the answers but I can provide a listening ear and may be able to point you in the direction of those with the appropriate skills and an open heart in your locality.

Printed in Great Britain
by Amazon

30437403R00044